W9-BVK-447

THE IRISH POTATO
FAMINE

Essential Events

THE IRISH POTATO FAMINE

BY JOSEPH R. O'NEILL

Content Consultant
Nicholas Wolf, PhD
Irish Studies
George Mason University

ABDO
Publishing Company

CREDITS

Editor: Nadia Higgins
Copy Editor: Paula Lewis
Interior Design and Production: Ryan Haugen/Nicole Brecke
Cover Design: Nicole Brecke

Library of Congress Cataloging-in-Publication Data
O'Neill, Joseph R.
  The Irish potato famine / by Joseph R. O'Neill.
    p. cm. — (Essential events)
  Includes bibliographical references and index.
  ISBN 978-1-60453-514-3
  1. Ireland—History—Famine, 1845-1852—Juvenile literature. 2.
Famines—Ireland—History—19th century—Juvenile literature. I.
Title.

  DA950.7.O54 2009
  941.5081—dc22

                          2008033107

TABLE OF CONTENTS

Beside a sculpture entitled "The Great Hunger Memorial," people observe a moment of silence during a St. Patrick's Day parade in New York City.

A Devastating Tragedy

In 1845, Great Britain was the wealthiest and most powerful nation in the world. The British ruled an empire that stretched across six continents. Its borders included parts of Africa and North America as well as Hong Kong, Australia, and

India. It was literally true that, well into the twentieth century, the sun never set on the British Empire.

Much closer to home, the British also controlled the island nation of Ireland. Here, less than 100 miles (160 km) west of Great Britain, the heart of this great empire, a tragedy of epic proportions began to unfold. Before its end, the tragedy would take approximately 1 million lives. It would chase more than 2 million people from their homeland. It would nearly erase a culture and language thousands of years old.

THE GREAT HUNGER

This tragedy is known as the Irish potato famine. Sometimes it is simply referred to as the Great Famine. Though people in Ireland speak English, many also speak the country's ancient, native language, Irish. In that language, the tragedy is known as *An Gorta Mór,* which means "The Great Hunger."

The Irish potato famine began in 1845 and ravaged the country

"We cannot undo the silence of our own past, but we can lend our voice to those who now suffer. . . . I have met children in schools and men and women all over Ireland who make an effortless and sympathetic connection between our past suffering and the present tragedies of hunger in the world. [T]he best possible commemoration of the men and women who died in that famine, who were cast up on other shores because of it, is to take their dispossession into the present with us, to help others who now suffer in a similar way."[1]
—*Ireland's president Mary Robinson, commemorating the 150th anniversary of the Great Famine in 1995*

until 1852. During this time, approximately one-
third of the country's people died or moved away.
Afterward, Ireland's population continued to drop
until as recently as the 1990s. Today, more than
150 years later, Ireland's population is approximately
half of what it was before the Great Famine. This
catastrophe is considered one of the most severe
famines of the modern era. The fact that it unfolded
on the doorstep of the world's richest nation makes
it even more devastating.

By the mid-1800s, the Irish had been living
for decades in extreme poverty, but the repeated
and total failure of the potato crop drove them to
tragedy. The Irish people suffered from extreme
hunger, which often led to illness. In turn, the sick
and dying could no longer afford to pay their rents.
They were forced off their lands, and their homes
were knocked down. Many of those who had been
driven out of their homes died in ditches along
country roads or in other lonely places. Newspapers
from the famine years tell about the bodies of
men, women, and children lying unburied along
the roadsides. They tell of gangs of roving beggars,
as thin as skeletons. And crime rates rose as the
desperate stole food from homes and stores.

In this 1846 illustration, a starving Irish boy and girl search for potatoes.

Many people committed theft in the open, hoping to be caught red-handed. They thought they would have better chances of surviving in jail or in British penal colonies, such as Australia, than at liberty in Ireland. Those who could afford to do so fled the country. Most of them went to the United States.

FAMINE IN THE MIDST OF PLENTY

A famine is a complex and deadly crisis initially caused by a widespread lack of food. In a famine, many people do die of starvation, but more commonly famine victims die from diseases that run rampant when a population is weakened by severe malnutrition.

However, a lack of food does not always result in a famine. In Ireland, the potato crops failed each year beginning in 1845 because of a plant disease called potato blight. The potato

Not a Distant Event

Though the Irish potato famine occurred overseas, it forever changed the course of U.S. history. Because of the Great Hunger, millions of Irish people fled their homeland. Most of them came to the United States, changing the character of the nation. Today, 40 million Irish Americans make up a highly successful portion of U.S. society.

The Irish also changed the religious makeup of the United States, which had been mostly Protestant. The Irish, followed later by Germans, Italians, Poles, and Mexicans, increased the number of the country's Catholics. Today, Catholicism is the largest religious denomination in the United States, with more than 71 million followers.

Perhaps the most significant change brought by the Irish was an appreciation for the role of immigrants. In the 1840s and 1850s, the United States was expanding westward. The Irish and other immigrant groups helped to fill the plains of the Midwest. They laid down railroad tracks, dug canals, and worked the thick black soil of the so-called Great American Desert.

The Irish, at first feared and hated by Americans, eventually showed the need for accepting new citizens from abroad. As the ships of Irish became fewer, Italians, Germans, Czechs, Poles, and Portuguese sought new homes in America. The Irish paved the way for these newcomers.

blight had also struck the United States and much of northern and central Europe. These places were far more populous than Ireland. Even so, they did not experience famines even remotely as destructive as Ireland's.

In fact, there *was* no lack of food in Ireland during the Great Famine. While millions starved, Ireland's farms produced a great abundance of crops other than potatoes. Wheat, oats, barley, pigs, sheep, and cows continued to be exported to England and other parts of the British Empire. The helpless and dying Irish poor stood by and watched as the bounty of their land was loaded aboard ships bound for foreign lands.

Causes of the Famine

How could it be that the failure of only one vegetable could cause so much agony, death, and displacement? Economic and political factors played a crucial role. These factors made the Irish people vulnerable to famine. They also drastically hindered the effort to save lives once the crisis began.

What were these devastating factors? First was Britain's harsh and oppressive rule over Ireland. The Irish people had been subject to centuries of official discrimination at the hands of their rulers. Many British leaders regarded the Irish people as less than human. This attitude stemmed in part from religious differences between England and Ireland. Another factor was Ireland's severe poverty. More than half the Irish people had no land of their own to farm. They worked for wealthy landlords. The Irish peasants tended to the country's richest land and grew crops destined to be exported. Even during the worst years of the famine, Great Britain ensured that Ireland's exports of grains and other crops continued uninterrupted. And so, most Irish people, reduced to such extreme poverty, came to depend on only one crop for their survival. This hearty crop, which grew easily in the island's poorest soil, was the potato.

"That one million people should have died in what was then part of the richest and most powerful nation in the world is something that still causes pain as we reflect on it today. Those who governed in London at the time failed their people through standing by while a crop failure turned into a massive human tragedy. We must not forget such a dreadful event."[2]

—Tony Blair, the British prime minister, speaking in 1997

A historical map shows the two main islands of Britain (right) and Ireland (left).

*A Celtic cross, the cross of early Christians of Ireland,
is an important landmark in the Irish village of Kells.*

HISTORY OF IRELAND

It is not clear who the first inhabitants of Ireland were and what their language and customs were like. However, evidence of prehistoric Irish peoples dates back more than 5,000 years. Ireland's early history describes the formation of a thriving, independent civilization. When British rule began in the twelfth century, Ireland's independence slowly eroded. The modern nation, the Republic of Ireland, did not gain its independence until 1921.

Celtic Rule to Catholicism

The Celts were a fierce, warlike group who came from mainland Europe. By 500 BCE, a tribe of Celts invaded the British Isles and conquered the Irish. The Celts intermarried with the native population of Ireland. The cultures mixed so thoroughly that, by the fourth century BCE, the pre-Celtic language of Ireland was mostly lost. The inhabitants spoke a unique variant of Celtic called Goidelic. This was an early form of the Gaelic, or Irish, language. In worship, they performed sacrifices—including human sacrifices—to many gods.

Prehistoric Tombs

Little is known about the prehistoric Irish. However, historians do know they built many curious burial monuments of earth and stone. One of the more famous of these is a so-called passage tomb at Newgrange. The tomb is an earthen mound that covers nearly one acre (0.4 ha) of land. A 62-foot (19-m) stone passageway leads to an inner chamber, which is also lined with stones. The tomb's entrance is also protected by gigantic stones. These had been cut from the earth and dragged into position from miles away. Some of the stones show mysterious carvings. It is estimated that the tomb took more than 20 years to complete.

In the first century of the common era, the Romans conquered Britain, but they never set their eye on Ireland. So Celtic religion and customs continued to thrive. The Romans and the Irish had little to do with each other. However, both civilizations did practice slavery, and each looked to the other as a source of slaves. Romans captured Celts in battles and sent the captives all over the Roman Empire to toil as slaves. Likewise, Celts periodically conducted raids against Roman settlements in

The Irish Language

The form of the Celtic language that evolved in Ireland is known as Gaelic, the language of the Gaels, or Irish Celts. When the Gaels entered what today is Scotland, they spread Gaelic there. Over time, Scots Gaelic and Irish Gaelic evolved into two separate dialects, or versions of the same language. The dialects have different spellings and pronunciations as well as words.

Today, Scots Gaelic is a minority language. Irish Gaelic, known simply as Irish, is the official and first language of the Republic of Ireland as well as an official language of the European Union. Despite this special status, however, less than half of Ireland's population has a command of the language. Even fewer people speak it on a regular basis.

Most Irish speak English. Because it was the language of the conquering British, English was favored in Ireland for many centuries. Adopting English became a way of improving one's social and economic status. Irish gradually fell out of everyday use.

Today the Irish government is committed to reviving Irish. Public signs are now written in both Irish and English. Irish language radio, television, and Web sites are growing. Some communities, known as *Gaeltachtaí*, are committed to only using Irish.

Britain and Gaul (France). They captured Romans and forced them into slavery.

In the fourth century CE, the Roman Empire—including Britain—adopted Christianity. By the next century, the Roman Empire was crumbling. Though still Romanized and Christian, by 410, Britain was no longer part of the Roman Empire. Without Roman support, Britain's defenses were weakened, and Celtic raids increased. The Celts captured even more British slaves, who now included some Christians. The most famous of these was a young man named Patrick. Later known as Saint Patrick, he is credited with uniting the Irish people under the Roman Catholic Church.

By the sixth century, Catholic Christianity had firmly taken hold throughout all of Ireland. Hundreds of Catholic monasteries were built on the island. They became important

Saint Patrick

Patrick was 16 when he was brought as a captive to Ireland. During his captivity, Patrick learned the Irish language and religion of his captors. However, his own Christian faith grew stronger. He began to have visions urging him to escape. After six years, he finally fled to northern Gaul, where he became a priest of the Roman Church.

Christian missionaries had been in Ireland for about a century. Some of the Celts had converted to Christianity, but had strayed from the teachings of the church. After Patrick was ordained a bishop, he went back to Ireland to spread Catholic teachings. In his missions throughout the north of Ireland, he used the shamrock to teach about the Trinity—a belief about the nature of God that is central to Catholic Christianity.

centers of production and trade, learning, and
the arts.

British Rule Begins

Ireland's long, tangled history with England
began in earnest in 1171. That year, King Henry II
of England officially incorporated Ireland as part of
his kingdom. For the next several centuries, English
kings devised a successful system for controlling
Ireland. They gave away Irish lands to English
noblemen and generals who had served the English
Crown loyally. In turn, they secured the loyalty of
Irish chieftains (minor kings who ruled over sections
of the island) by granting them special privileges
and land. In this fashion, the English were able to
gradually extend their control over the island.

The English noblemen took pains never to adopt
the ways and language of the Irish. For their part,
the chieftains increasingly adopted English fashions
and the English language as their own. As time
progressed, the culture and language of England
became fashionable, while Irish culture came to be
considered rude and backward.

In 1534, King Henry VIII of England broke away
from the Roman Catholic Church. He founded

The remains of medieval Irish monasteries are some of Ireland's most cherished historical sites today.

the Church of England, a Protestant religion, in its place. The people of England were forced to abandon the Roman Church. Henry closed down Ireland's monasteries and destroyed many in the process. Much of the wealth from these ruined monasteries was given over to landholders in Ireland in return for their continued loyalty to England and to its new church. However, since the landholders in Ireland had become so distant from their subjects, England's changes of religious policy had little effect on the common Irish peasants. They continued to practice Catholicism.

IRELAND AS A BRITISH COLONY

Before Queen Mary I of England assumed power in 1553, English settlers were not widespread in Ireland. The English and their descendants lived mostly in a small region surrounding the city of Dublin. A new phase of English colonization of the island began during Mary's rule. The queen, a Catholic, encouraged settlers to extend their reach in Ireland. Her successor, Elizabeth I, further encouraged this process. However, unlike Mary, Elizabeth was a staunch Protestant. For her, the issue was about more than just land. She began to harshly persecute Irish Catholics as well.

In the north, Irish chieftains rose up against British rule. After several years, their rebellion was put down by Elizabeth's successor, James I, in 1603. James then seized the defeated chieftains' lands. The land was turned over to thousands of settlers from England and Scotland, who streamed into the island between 1607 and 1641.

In 1641, Catholics in Ireland staged another revolt against the Protestant English Crown.

By 1649, however, a military commander and staunch Protestant named Oliver Cromwell had risen to power in England. He invaded Ireland, slaughtering thousands of people in response to the Catholic uprising of 1641. He also sent away more than 100,000 Irish to England's new American colonies.

When Cromwell died in 1658, the British monarchy was restored. However, the heir to the throne, James II, was a Catholic. He was soon forced out of power. The fiercely Protestant William of Orange was crowned. The deposed King James fled to Ireland to seek help to win back his throne. The Irish people stood with James in battle against England in 1690, but William soundly defeated James's army.

THE PENAL LAWS

After the battle, Ireland's Protestants looked for a way to

Northern Ireland

Ireland is an island approximately the size of Indiana. The relatively small island is divided into two parts politically. The Republic of Ireland was born under the terms of a 1949 treaty with Great Britain. This country takes up the majority of the island. The northernmost part of the island is called Northern Ireland. This remains part of the United Kingdom today. Both regions suffered from the Great Famine.

keep further Catholic uprisings at bay. In 1695, they introduced the Penal Laws. These laws aimed to discourage as much as possible the practice of the Catholic religion. It also forbade Catholics to purchase or inherit land. Catholics could not vote, hold any public office, practice law, serve in the army, or own a gun or a sword. Churches and schools were closed down, making it very difficult for Catholics to obtain even the most basic education.

By 1829, when the last of the Penal Laws were finally repealed, less than 5 percent of Irish farms were owned by native, Catholic-Irish people. A small number of Anglo-Irish landlords (Protestant landlords of English descent) owned almost all of Ireland. The vast majority of Irish toiled on tiny plots of rented land. They eked out just barely enough to survive.

The people who could boast of an ancient culture steeped in learning and the arts were now reduced to a colony of servants. Morale was low; poverty and illiteracy were high. Ireland was at its lowest point ever. It was these conditions that made the people so vulnerable to failures of the potato crops in the middle 1800s.

Irish peasant children from the 1800s carry blocks of peat (a type of fuel) to pay for school.

An Irish family farms a small plot of rocky, mountainous land.

ON THE BRINK
OF DISASTER

Many of those who owned Ireland's land never set foot on their estates. Often, their vast estates were divided among middle-class Irish farmers called middlemen, who then subdivided the land among tenants and laborers.

MIDDLEMEN, TENANTS, AND LABORERS

The middlemen paid rent to the landlords, who, in turn, profited from the land. The middlemen hired laborers to work the best fields. They rented poorer land to tenant farmers. As part or even all of their wages, some of the laborers were granted a small plot of land, often as small as one-fourth acre (0.1 ha). This arrangement was called conacre. On a bit of the country's poorest land, a laborer could build a cottage and grow potatoes.

The Worth of an Acre

Most Irish farms in the middle 1800s were less than 20 acres (8 ha), and many were just one acre (0.4 ha). Those who worked for conacre often were forced to get by on one-half acre (0.2 ha) or even one-fourth acre (0.1 ha). An acre is slightly smaller than a football field. This might sound like a lot of land, but it was not. It provided no margin of error for a family that had to grow an entire year's worth of food from it.

Other workers were seasonal help, paid a low wage at planting or harvesting time. These migrant workers often had no place to call their own. They slept outdoors as they traveled the countryside year-round. Other laborers worked their own conacre plots part of the year. The rest of the time, they tried to make ends meet by working elsewhere while their wives and children tended the home crops.

Tenant farmers were slightly better off than laborers. Their plots were usually 20 acres (8 ha)

Farming Weather

Ireland enjoys a maritime, temperate climate with cool summers and mild winters. The average summer temperature is 60° Fahrenheit (16°C). In winter, the average temperature is 42° Fahrenheit (6°C). It rains a lot in Ireland, with the average annual rainfall at more than 40 inches (102 cm). However, rain comes and goes in short bursts. It usually rains at least once every day, which is why Ireland is so green. In fact, one nickname for Ireland is "the Emerald Isle." Snow falls occasionally in midwinter. However, except for in the mountains, snowfall rarely lasts for more than a few hours. Total precipitation varies across the island significantly. The west of Ireland is far cooler and wetter than the southeast, which enjoys the most sunshine.

or smaller. These farmers raised animals and grew their own crops of wheat and other grains. They sold their harvest in order to pay their rents. Like laborers, they also grew potatoes on marginal land for themselves. However, tenants were able to supplement their diet with whatever was left over after paying rent. Tenant farmers often also subdivided their plots. They rented out the poorest land to laborers who worked in exchange for a place to build a hut and grow potatoes.

In 1845, approximately 4 to 6 million people in Ireland lived on tiny plots of land. They struggled to pay their rents to the middlemen, or they toiled on another family's plot in return for conacre. These people accounted for one-half of Ireland's population. And they all depended on one crop—the potato—for a major portion of their diet. Of these 4 to 6 million people, more than

3.3 million ate nothing but the potato, occasionally with buttermilk and salt.

THE IMPORTANCE OF THE POTATO

Ireland's best land was reserved for growing grain for the landlords. So the many poor were forced to grow their own food in thin, rocky soil or on mountainsides. The Irish came to depend so very much on the potato because it is a hearty crop. Even on tiny patches of poor soil, a family could grow plenty of potatoes to feed themselves for most of the year.

Though a diet of potatoes may have been boring,

Peasant Homes

Most Irish tenants and laborers lived in one-room cottages. These were built with mud walls. The roofs were made out of a thick layer of dried grass, called thatch. More fortunate families lived in stone cottages that most often had dirt floors and thatched roofs.

Peasants relied on fires to cook and heat their homes. Since Ireland did not have forests, fires were not fueled with wood. Instead, peasants burned peat, or lumps of decayed swamp vegetation, which gave off a thick, oily smoke. A one-room cottage did not have a chimney or windows. That meant that the unpleasant smoke lingered in the room, as it slowly escaped through the thatched roof.

Peasants could not afford separate barns, so the family's pig and chickens shared their single room. Outside the door stood a pile of manure. This was saved for use as fertilizer for the potatoes.

Many people lacked furniture, too. A study of residents of County Donegal in 1837 found that 9,000 people owned a total of 10 beds, 93 chairs, and 243 stools. Most of Ireland's population slept on dirt floors with their family and, if they were lucky, the pig.

A scene from the Irish town of Galway shows what rural life was like during the famine years.

it kept the Irish people relatively healthy and strong, especially when the potato was dipped in buttermilk. Buttermilk is a by-product of the butter-making process. Most Irish people could not afford to raise a cow or buy butter or fresh milk. However, those who were fortunate enough to keep a cow would make butter and sell it to wealthier people. In the days before refrigeration, there was no reliable way to preserve milk. Most milk was churned into butter or made into cheese. Although butter and cheese were expensive, the by-product, buttermilk, was not. Buttermilk was a fortunate addition to the Irish diet because it provided the nutrients, such as fats and vitamin A, that the potato lacked.

Potatoes were typically boiled and then eaten with the hands. The tough skin was peeled away with the thumbnail and discarded. Women in County Donegal even wove special pouches for their husbands to carry mashed potatoes in while the men worked in the fields. Families fortunate enough to have a pig or chickens fed their animals potatoes, too.

MEAL MONTHS

If the potato crop were to fail for some reason, it would spell disaster. And fail it did, on occasion. With either too much or too little rain, or in very cold years, or in certain areas, there were poor harvests. However, these scanty harvests were short-lived and regional. People would go hungry, but the strong survived on meager meals of oatmeal or a neighbor's stores. Generally, only the very old and the very young suffered. Most people lived to eat next year's potatoes.

However, even in a season of good weather, the poorest people were forced to go hungry every year, during the so-called meal months. From June through August, the potato plants were too young to produce food. During this time, a pig could be sold or slaughtered for meat. Those who could afford to do so purchased oatmeal or meal made from "Indian corn," or maize. But those who did not own a pig and could not afford meal went without. They survived on a meager diet of fish, garden vegetables, and seaweed while they anxiously awaited the first potatoes in the early fall.

However, what began in 1845 was a new form of hardship. This was the beginning of a series of total potato-crop failures all over Ireland. There would not be a fortunate neighbor to ask for potatoes. Nor would there be a crop to look forward to the next year. And even as the population grew desperate, Ireland's abundant grains and other crops remained off-limits due to complex economic and political factors. Ending the potato blight was the Irish peasants' only hope.

An Irish farmer and his wife plant potatoes circa 1935.
The scene accurately depicts rural life in the mid-1800s.

A modern-day Irish farmer digs up potatoes. Today, farmers use fungicides
to prevent the blight that devastated Ireland during the famine.

An Spáinneach,
the Potato

he potato, *Solanum tuberosum,* is the plant and
the edible tubers it produces. A tuber is a
part of the root that stores starches and sugars. The
plant relies on the tuber to grow during the winter
and to reproduce.

The dark green, leafy plant can grow upward of three feet (0.9 m). It produces white or purple flowers and inedible berries the size of cherries. The plant is poisonous. Eating the stem, leaves, or berries can make a human ill, and it can kill small animals. However, it is the edible tuber that made *Solanum tuberosum* famous.

THE POTATO COMES TO IRELAND

Ireland's most important plant was, in fact, a native of South America. Long before the Great Famine, the potato had been cultivated by American Indians. It was a staple crop for those living in the Andes Mountains, in what is today Peru. The Spanish learned about the benefits of this food during their conquests of the Americas. They brought potatoes back to Europe in the late 1500s or early 1600s. That is why some Irish poets called the potato

The Word *Potato*

The word *potato* comes from the Spanish word *patata*. This, in turn, is a Spanish spelling of a Native-American word for the vegetable, *batata*. The Irish variably called the potato *potáta, fata, prata,* or the English potato. They also used the nickname "spud," which stemmed from an old word for a type of knife used to dig up potatoes.

an Spáinneach (an-spawn-ACK), or the Spaniard.

The potato spread slowly throughout Europe in the 1600s. It was used mainly as food for animals and for making alcoholic beverages. Poorer families were the first to plant potatoes along with other vegetables. The potato was intended as a supplement to traditional meals or as a food of last resort during lean times.

By some accounts, the potato was first introduced into Ireland in the first half of the seventeenth century. For the first 60 years, it was planted only sparsely. One source, written in 1664, sings the vegetable's praises:

> [Potatoes] . . . thrive and prosper very well in Ireland, where there is whole Fields of them. . . . They are in quality temperate, very agreeable and amicable to the Nature of Man, and of a good and strong nourishment. [1]

A Food Worthy of Celebration

This wedding song from 1674 indicates that the potato was not always considered a lowly peasant food. When the vegetable was first introduced in Ireland, it was thought of as a delicacy. Part of the song is:

". . . Whereas it was kisses
With formality
Or a potato
That used to salute her
Before their marriage."[2]

Eventually, the Irish recognized the potato as a healthy vegetable—and one that grew well in Ireland's rocky and sandy soil. By the late seventeenth century, the potato was a staple of Irish agriculture. By the early nineteenth century, poorer families were becoming more and more dependent on the potato alone.

THE "IRISH POTATO"

The white potato became known to the outside world as the "Irish potato." English cartoons of the nineteenth century went so far as to draw Irish people as potatoes.

For almost two centuries, potatoes grew reliably year after year, with only a few exceptions. The hearty food fueled the Irish population. As potatoes became plentiful, the Irish population exploded. From 1750 to 1840, the population of Ireland more than tripled from approximately 2.6 million to approximately 8.5 million. Some of the increase may be due in part to better methods of counting the population. Nevertheless, the potato certainly deserves much of the credit.

However, the rise of both the potato and the population was not uniform across Ireland.

This happened most rapidly in the west and southwest provinces, the country's poorest areas. The Irish peasantry benefited the most from the potato because it produced more food per acre than any other crop available to them. Since the poorest people had been banished to the country's least-suitable land, the stubborn potato became their main food source.

However, Ireland's poor would be the most severely affected should the potato crops fail—which is what happened beginning in the fall of 1845. After the long "meal

"Lazy Beds"

The British planted their potatoes in neat, narrow rows using a horse-drawn plow. The Irish method was quite different. The English called it the "lazy bed" method. Despite its name, however, the lazy bed method was well suited to Irish soils and weather.

Farmers used some of the previous years' crops for seeds, which had been stored in underground pits. These potatoes were planted either with a spade or by hand in broad rows called beds. A bed could be up to one yard (0.9 m) wide. A narrow trench was dug on either side of the bed. The trenches gave the farmers access to the plants, which proved helpful for weeding. They also allowed excess rainwater to drain off.

When the potatoes were ready to be harvested, the lazy beds were dug up with spades. Each potato was then picked by hand. Usually, one potato crop would yield two different harvests. The first potatoes were ready in late September and early October; the so-called late crop was ready by late November and early December.

The lazy bed method worked well in rocky, wet soil and even on slopes. It allowed the "lazy" Irish to put even the most marginal land under the potato.

months," the hungry peasants eagerly grabbed their shovels and dug for the first crop of potatoes. Instead of potatoes, though, one farmer after another across Ireland turned up shovelfuls of smelly, slimy mud.

A MYSTERIOUS DISEASE

The life-giving potato had fallen victim to a mysterious disease that turned the potato's green leaves black. It turned the spuds into mud. Even the best British scientists could not explain it. Only in later decades would scientists identify the cause of the so-called potato blight. The cause was a disease caused by the fungus *Phytophthora infestans,* a type of microorganism related to mushrooms and mold. Some scientists believe that the fungus came from South America on ships carrying cargo into European ports. Others suspect that the deadly disease came from the eastern United States, where a potato blight had destroyed crops in 1843 and 1844.

By the summer of 1845, the blight had spread over northern and central Europe. Belgium, Holland, France, and southern England were the first hit, followed by Germany and Poland. The first reports of blight in Ireland came in September. On September 13, 1845, the *Gardener's Chronicle* conveyed the panic this news understandably caused:

> We stop the Press with very great regret to announce that the
> potato [blight] has unequivocally declared itself in Ireland.
> The crops about Dublin are suddenly perishing. . . . Where
> will Ireland be in the event of a universal potato rot?[3]

The fungus grew on the underside of an infected plant's blackened and shriveled leaves. When the wind blew, it released millions of spores, or tiny seedlike particles, into the air. Carried by the winds, the fungus spread from plant to plant. But the blight did not just affect growing crops. Harvested potatoes stored for food or seeds for the following year also turned to mud. The stench of rotting potatoes wafted throughout Ireland.

*A newspaper illustration from 1849 shows a poor Irish family
searching for potatoes in a field.*

Approximately 10,000 victims of the famine were buried, many of them in mass graves, at the Abbeystrewery Cemetery in Ireland.

AN GORTA MÓR, THE GREAT HUNGER

s the potato blight spread throughout Ireland in the early autumn of 1845, there was little fear of famine. British and Irish agricultural experts expressed concern about a potential disaster, but the people were confident in their hearty spud. More acres had been devoted to the potato than ever before. Surely, the total destruction of all potatoes in Ireland was out of the question. Also, oats had grown unusually well the previous summer and were extremely plentiful.

Panic Spreads

In November, the late potato crops were ready for harvest. When farmers dug, however, they were met with a chilling realization: the blight persisted. Letters from clergymen and middlemen to landlords and government officials began to hint of panic throughout the countryside. In December, the *Freeman's Journal* reported that at least half of Ireland's potatoes were "already lost as human food."[1] Mysteriously, even healthy potatoes rotted soon after having been put into storage. People feared that by January there would be no potatoes left to eat.

Newspaper reports about early famine-related deaths were widely read in Ireland and England. However, most officials in London stubbornly refused to believe that people were dying of starvation so close to the heart of their great empire. The government requested proof that people were indeed dying from hunger and

An Agonizing Process

Death by starvation is a slow and agonizing process. Once nutrients no longer enter the body, the body breaks down its own fat and muscle in order to keep the brain and heart functioning.

In addition to extreme weakness, severe malnutrition causes a number of painful and deadly symptoms. Starving people often appear to have big bellies, as fluid builds up in the abdomen. Also, the lack of vitamins causes several disorders. These include anemia (a shortage of iron, which is necessary for the blood to carry oxygen to the body); scurvy (a shortage of vitamin C that causes bruising, sore joints, and bleeding from the gums); and pellagra (a protein and vitamin B deficiency resulting in sensitivity to light, diarrhea, skin sores, mental illness, and death).

not from other, unrelated causes. One of the first famine victims was Denis McKennedy. British officials demanded that his corpse be cut open to examine the contents of his stomach. Only bits of undigested plant leaves, stalks, and roots were found in McKennedy's digestive system.

As history would show, officials in London were tragically slow to react to the alarming reports from Ireland. Relief had begun in the late fall of 1845 with the founding of the Central Relief Commission in November. This group oversaw food depots that were set up to sell cheap maize, or Indian corn. As the famine progressed, the commission would help organize public works projects that offered some jobs. In the worst years, it ran soup kitchens and workhouses. However, those efforts were deeply flawed. Projects were begun and then stopped, due to political changes in London. Philosophical ideas about how the relief should be handled led to disastrous policy decisions. Relief would be too late and too little for many millions of Irish people.

The Crop of 1846

By the spring of 1846, the potato blight was ravishing Ireland, but full-fledged famine was still at bay. Hunger and sickness gripped the land, but there were no reports of mass death.

The potato crop in the fall of 1846 was harvested with much anticipation. The hungry people had spent the year with far less food than was normal, but most people survived. Their hopes were high. As they dug, their potatoes again came up as smelly sludge. Panic gave way to desperation as millions across Ireland realized that the coming year would bring even less food.

Tragic Stories

By winter, there was little doubt that people were dying of starvation. Early in 1847—the worst year of the famine—reported deaths multiplied. By spring, stories about famine deaths had become so common that newspapers stopped reporting them. Visitors from abroad reported bands of ghostlike beggars stumbling along the main roads. Corpses littered the highways and gutters of small towns and villages. So many people died that it was no longer possible to provide everyone with proper burials. Mass graves were dug, and gangs were recruited by local authorities to collect bodies and toss them into the freshly dug pits.

Many of the Irish died of starvation, while others died of illness. Starvation weakens the body's immune systems, which are the

Cherished Rituals

Before the famine, the Irish people observed a number of rituals to mark the passing of a loved one. The two major ceremonies were the wake and the funeral. At a wake, friends and family gathered to mourn their loss but also to celebrate their loved one's life. Mourners displayed a wide range of emotions. They might wail with grief or engage in lively song and dance.

The funeral was more formal. This was a full Mass in a church, where all the ritual splendor of the Catholic faith was on display. Burning incense gave off perfumed smoke, and priests in decorated vestments chanted prayers. Afterward, mourners proceeded to the graveyard with the coffin. They sang prayers over the body as it was lowered into the grave.

There was so much death during the famine years that most of these cherished rituals were set aside. Loved ones were tossed—sometimes still barely alive—into mass graves. Many starving people ended up at prisonlike workhouses. Here, deaths were so frequent that many bodies were placed in caskets with hinged bottoms. At mass graves, the bottom of the casket was opened like a door. The body was dumped, and the casket was returned to the workhouse to be reused. For the Irish, such unceremonious burials were the saddest realities of the famine years.

body's natural protections against disease. Also, a starving person lacks the strength to bathe or clean up, so germs are abundant and spread easily. The famine also prompted people to flee from the countryside to crowded cities and workhouses in search of help. The crowded conditions further encouraged the spread of diseases. In particular, officials in Dublin were overwhelmed with reports of dysentery, a highly contagious disease that causes severe diarrhea, intestinal bleeding, and death.

Black '47

The worst year of the famine came to be known as Black '47. Civil unrest and occasional rioting spread through the once-peaceful countryside. The casualties mounted. In the confusion of the stench, suffering, and sickness, sometimes the barely still-living were tossed

"Death is in every hovel, disease and famine are affecting the young and old, the strong and weak, the mother and the infant. The husband dies by the side of the wife and she doesn't realise that he has died. The same rags cover the skeletons of the dead and the skeleton shape of the living. Rats devour the corpse and there is no energy among the living to drive them from their horrid feast."[2]
—The Cork Examiner, *1846*

An illustration from 1847 shows destitute Irish peasants inside a ruined cottage.

into communal graves. Entire families shuttered themselves inside their huts, and, too weak to move, the living slept next to the dead. Grass grew high in front of cottage doors, as nobody was coming in and out and no animals were grazing. The families within wasted away to nothing.

Starvation caused psychological disorders as well. People became depressed, paranoid, and hysterical. Long-married couples regarded each other as complete strangers, while young couples, newly in love, eyed each other with suspicion. Starving people also felt intense sensitivity to light and noise. Perhaps this helps explains why one family barricaded themselves in their cottage until they died. They were found some time later. The men who discovered them "got weak and sick and had to be given whiskey" in order to recover from the sight.[3]

Entire villages and towns were completely devastated. The residents were either dead or, unable to pay rent, had been evicted by their landlords. Some people hid the bodies of their family, friends, and neighbors for weeks. They hoped to claim the deceased's food rations that were handed out by the government as part of its meager relief efforts. Travelers reported seeing half-starved dogs gnawing on the emaciated limbs of their dead owners. Such were the horrific scenes of suffering and chaos as 1 million people perished for want of food.

Dashed Hopes

The potato harvest of the fall of 1847 was slightly improved over previous years. However, with so many sick and dead, fewer potatoes had been planted. Also, the potato blight had seriously reduced the number of seeds available for planting.

A mural in Belfast, Northern Ireland, portrays three suffering women digging for potatoes during the Great Famine.

Those who had managed to get in a good crop rejoiced. Perhaps the potato blight had left Ireland.

The slightly better harvests of 1847 led to a decline in deaths in 1848. The hopeful and desperate survivors turned out in full force in the summer of 1848 to plant potatoes. They joyfully expected an end to the Great Hunger.

As the first crops of 1848 were dug up, however, the hopes of the Irish were horribly dashed. The blight was back. The crops that had been planted under great strain and toil were turning up shovelfuls of rot. The spirit of the Irish people was broken. The suffering of late 1848 and 1849 matched, if not bested, the misery of Black '47.

THE END OF THE FAMINE

It is difficult to state exactly when the Great Famine ended. Deaths were reduced and agriculture was revived at different rates and at different times across Ireland. However, historians generally mark 1852 as the last year of the Great Famine. Though the famine ended, the lot of the Irish did not improve significantly until many years later. Tens of thousands of people continued to leave Ireland for distant lands. Also, with so many people dead or gone from Ireland, it is difficult to say that the famine had truly run its course. Because potato production remained low, overall food levels of 1852 were significantly

"Three Grains of Corn, Mother"

Amelia Blanford Edwards was an English writer born in 1831. Though she was born in London, her mother was Irish. Edwards wrote "Three Grains of Corn, Mother" from the point of view of a starving boy during the Great Famine. The poem begins by describing the boy's agony. Soon it takes a scathing tone as the boy says, "There is many a brave heart here, Mother, dying of want and cold, / While only across the Channel [in England], Mother, are many that roll in gold; / There are rich and proud men there, Mother, with wonderous wealth to view, / And the bread they fling to their dogs tonight would give life to me and you."[4]

lower than those of even 1846. Perhaps there simply were not significant numbers of poor people left to fall victim to starvation. The fact of the matter remains that by 1852, approximately 3 million Irish had either died or moved away.

An "Artificial" Famine?

Some historians contend that the Great Famine was an "artificial" famine. Ireland was producing enough wheat, oats, and other food during the famine years to feed its population. Why was there a famine at all?

As in many other cases, the presence of food alone is not enough to keep famine away. The Irish had become so dependent upon the potato that, when it failed, there were no substitutes. Much of Ireland's wheat, oat, and other crops were exported overseas. However, some of these crops were sold at local Irish markets. The Irish poor simply could not afford to buy them. This situation was worsened by a key principle of capitalism: When many people desire a specific good (for example, food during a famine) and its supply remains limited, the price of the good goes up. And so, the famine drove up prices of these desperately needed crops.

Even if the Irish poor could have afforded the crops, they had no access to them. Those hardest hit by famine were isolated in the west and southwest of the island. The main sources of food crops were in the center and southeast. There was no way to distribute the food around the island. The entire system of transport had evolved in Ireland to move goods and people from the center to ports at the southern, northern, and eastern edges. It would have required an incredible amount of organization and tremendous resources to reroute the flow of foodstuffs around Ireland so that those suffering the most could find relief.

These facts raise important issues. The British government did not take an active role in relieving the suffering. It did not stop exports or take action to make Ireland's bounty affordable. It did not seize Irish crops and distribute them throughout

"Famine and Exportation"

The following excerpt is from a poem by John O'Hagan, from between 1850 and 1890. Written in the voice of Irish peasants, it is directed at Great Britain. It expresses anger at the country's lack of help during the Great Famine:

"We are poor, and ye are rich; / Mind it not, were every ditch / Strewn in spring with famished corpses, / Take our oats to feed your horses!"[5]

the island. Why? The answers stem from disastrous philosophical and economic ideas that were popular in Britain at the time of the famine.

The skeletal figures in Dublin's famine memorial remind modern Irish
people of their country's past suffering.

A landowner on horseback evicts peasants who cannot pay their rent. British rulers did little to prevent mass evictions of Irish peasants.

GREAT BRITAIN'S ROLE

In the midst of Ireland's tragedy, Great Britain was in a position to relieve much of the misery. However, economic philosophies and political ideologies won out over humanitarianism. The powerful nation did little to help.

This was the case even though, at least officially, Ireland had stopped being a colony of Great Britain's in 1801. Ireland had been elevated to the position of a full-fledged member of the United Kingdom. The UK Flag (also known as the Union Jack) reflected this change. The Cross of Saint Patrick, an Irish symbol, was added to its design. However, Irish union with Great Britain was only a legal formality. The Irish were still treated as inferiors by the British. When it came to famine relief, the Union mattered very little.

A Policy of Laissez-Faire

Why did the British refuse to help? The ruling elite in London believed in the economic policies of laissez-faire capitalism. *Laissez-faire* is a French term that literally means "let him do as he will." In economics, it refers to the belief that government should never interfere with economic affairs. Therefore, those who believed in laissez-faire capitalism objected to government interference in the trade between England and Ireland.

Ireland's plentiful harvests of grain and other crops continued to be exported from Ireland during the famine years. Some people pressed the British

The Role of Charities

The government was un-willing to help the Irish people, but what about other groups? Donations poured in from charities around the world, includ-ing Britain, France, the United States, and India. The most notable charity during the famine years was the Society of Friends, or the Quakers. The group operated soup kitchens in Ireland through 1846 and Black '47.

However, as the fam-ine continued, "donor fatigue" set in. As in the case with disasters today, a feeling of helplessness took over. Charitable do-nations declined by 1847, and world attention was focused elsewhere.

Furthermore, by 1847, middle-class donors in Britain often shared their government's views about the Irish learning to stand on their own. Britain relied on the Poor Law system to take care of the problem.

to stop the exports. They believed the crops should stay on the island to feed the starving. However, such action was considered government interference in the "rights" of the wealthy landlords to do as they saw fit with the produce from their lands. If a landlord wanted to stop exporting his wheat, he was free to do so. But if the landlord wanted to make a profit from his wheat, that also was his right—even if the people harvesting it were starving.

Despite the sheer number of deaths due to starvation, the British government did not stop the food exports. Rather, many Irish peasants starved as the bounty of the Irish soil was loaded aboard ships bound for overseas markets. The British government sent in soldiers to guard the convoys that carried the grain from the fields to the port. At port, the Royal Navy protected the food-laden ships.

THE CORN LAWS

Since Ireland was, officially, in union with Great Britain, it was also subject to the so-called Corn Laws that applied to all grains. The Corn Laws had been enacted in 1815. They placed tariffs, or taxes, on foreign grain to be imported into the United Kingdom—which included Ireland. The idea was to protect British and Irish farmers from competition from, for example, German and U.S. farmers. The combination of laissez-faire capitalism and the Corn Laws hurt early relief efforts in Ireland. The British encouraged Irish crops to be exported. At the same time, the government made it expensive to import food from the United States and Europe to feed the Irish.

Britain's prime minister, Sir Robert Peel, worked to repeal, or take away, the Corn Laws. He opposed them for humanitarian reasons. He wished to enable cheap imports and lower food prices in Ireland during the famine. However, Peel's motives were political as well. His party strongly supported laissez-faire free trade—and the Corn Laws contradicted this policy of no interference. In 1846, Peel was successful, and the Corn Laws were repealed. One month later, however, he was forced to resign from power. Nevertheless, the repeal of the Corn Laws did help encourage imports and price drops.

Sir Charles Edward Trevelyan

Sir Charles Edward Trevelyan was the assistant secretary of the British Treasury under Peel. In this role, he held an extraordinary amount of power over Britain's finances. After Peel left office in 1846, Trevelyan took a greater role in the handling of famine relief. His approach differed significantly from Peel's. Trevelyan was a strict follower of laissez-faire capitalism. He also held personal ideas about the Irish people that affected his policy.

Trevelyan supported the idea of moralism, which was popular during the Great Famine. Trevelyan and many other upper-class Britons believed that the famine was a result of a moral defect within the Irish people. According to Trevelyan's

National Irish Famine Museum

Strokestown Park House was once the home of a wealthy Irish landlord. Today, it is the home of the National Irish Famine Museum. The site is typical of houses built by landlords in Ireland. Tunnels connect the manor house and several outbuildings as passageways for servants. This ensured the family's view of Strokestown Park was not hindered by the sight of servants. The kitchen is ringed by a balcony. The lady of the house gave orders to her servants from the balcony without coming in direct contact with them.

Sir Charles Trevelyan was the British official in charge of relief efforts in Ireland during much of the Great Famine.

view, the Irish were lazy, stupid, and immoral. They had brought the famine upon themselves. The so-called moralists believed that the Irish were, as a people, too dependent on others. If Great Britain gave free aid to the Irish, they argued, the Irish would take advantage of the situation. They would refuse to work, accepting welfare paid for by the hardworking English people. The moralists went so far as to suggest that the Irish would have more children just to increase the amount of their handouts. Trevelyan said that the real evil was not the famine itself but "the moral evil of the selfish, perverse, and turbulent character of the [Irish] people."[1]

WORKHOUSES

By the summer of 1847, government-run soup kitchens were supporting as many as 3 million people a day. By the fall of 1847, Trevelyan and British officials began closing down the soup kitchens. In an effort to end "handouts" and begin "relief," they decided to rely exclusively on Ireland's "Poor Law" system. This system had been in place since 1838. It was funded solely by local taxes, paid by Irish tenants and landlords. From Trevelyan's point of view, the Poor Law system was a way

Public Works Programs

In addition to the workhouses, some public works programs existed in Ireland during the famine. Irish peasants built roads or dug ditches for a minimum wage. However, these projects were physically demanding, and many of the workers were too weak from starvation to perform them. Furthermore, Trevelyan insisted that the wages be paid not by the hour but according to the amount of work accomplished. Therefore, the weakest and sickest— the ones who needed food the most—were paid the least. Many of the public works were so poorly run that many roads were built going from nowhere to no place in particular.

An 1846 illustration shows starving peasants clamoring to be admitted to an already overpopulated workhouse.

to make the Irish take responsibility for their own disaster. Unfortunately, Irish landlords and tenants became increasingly bankrupt by 1847. When they could not pay taxes, local relief efforts stopped.

The Poor Law system involved a network of workhouses. The workhouses originally had been intended to provide shelter to those who could not work, such as orphans, widows, the elderly, and the disabled. In 1847, the workhouses were open to the starving masses. But conditions at the workhouses were so bad that some took their chances at dying rather than enter one.

In the workhouses, the poor were fed, clothed—and "disciplined." In return, they performed grueling, monotonous labor. The workhouses were built like prisons, with bars over windows and surrounded by high stone walls.

Families who entered the workhouses were separated according to age and gender. Men, women, boys, and girls slept in separate dormitories. They ate in separate mess halls and exercised in separate yards. Families saw each other only during religious services on Sunday.

During the famine, the British government tried to limit the number of people in the workhouses. In order to keep the poor away, the work was designed to be as miserable as possible. The goal of the workhouse was to "discipline" the poor, to teach them the value of a meal through hard physical labor. Men replaced mules and horses in the backbreaking work of turning mills. Men, women, and children also wielded sledgehammers, breaking stones into gravel. They chopped wood and dug ditches. At one point, inmates crushed animal bones into powder for fertilizer. However, this task was stopped after guards discovered that workers were eating the bone dust.

As the starving and sick poured in, the workhouses became overcrowded, which helped spread disease. The workhouses became places of mass death. Life in them was so miserable that many people refused to become part of them. Many families did not want to be split up. They roamed the highways and the countryside, begging for food and eating whatever washed up on the beaches.

Natural Disaster or Genocide?

Great Britain stood alone as Ireland's only hope. Not only did that powerful nation fail its neighbor, it encouraged policies that perpetuated the suffering and mass death. For that reason, Ireland's hatred toward Britain was high after the famine. Irish Nationalists called for independence from the United Kingdom. Many, such as John Mitchel, accused the British of genocide—the deliberate killing of an entire people. Mitchel called the British relief efforts, the workhouses, and mass evictions "contrivances for slaughter."[2]

Today, most historians agree that, while the reactions—or inaction—of the British government were deadly, to call it genocide is an overstatement. As historian Peter Gray wrote, the mass deaths were not intentional:

The charge of culpable neglect of the consequences of policies leading to mass starvation is indisputable. . . . [However, it] was not a policy of deliberate genocide, but a dogmatic refusal to recognise that measures intended 'to encourage industry, to do battle with sloth and despair, to awake a manly feeling of inward confidence and reliance on the justice of heaven,' were based on false premises, and in the Irish conditions of the later 1840s amounted to a sentence of death on many thousands.[3]

"Benefits" of the Famine

Many Britons, including Trevelyan, justified their economic beliefs with religious ones. In their view, the famine was God's way of punishing the Irish people for their poor morals and laziness.

Some British administrators took this view even further. They believed that the Great Famine was actually a blessing that would correct the mismanagement of estates by Irish landlords. Irish farming methods at the time of the famine were inefficient and outdated. The British elite saw the division of Irish land among middlemen, then among tenants and laborers, as an obstacle to modernization. For years, they had wanted all the tenant farmers removed to consolidate land into larger farms. Food production would become much more efficient, productive, and, therefore, profitable. However, there had been no way of removing the 3 million or so excess farmers. In the eyes of some British, God sent the potato blight, and the issue was resolved. With millions of Irish people dying or leaving, the wealthy landlords were, for a time, finding their estates more manageable and profitable. To Trevelyan and others, the Great Hunger was "an economic miracle in the making."[4]

Mass Evictions

As if death and emigration were not enough, evictions were another way for the wealthy landowners to clear the land of unwanted farmers. During the Great Famine, millions of tenant farmers and laborers had been unable to pay rent. They were either too weak to toil for the landlords and middlemen, or they had eaten their rents in desperation. Landlords began mass evictions; millions of people were forced off the lands they had worked. Their cottages were knocked down, and the peasants were sent off with only what they could carry. Now the landlord could further consolidate his lands.

What happened to those who were evicted? As Ireland's poorest people, they could not afford food and clothing, let alone passage to the New World. Most of the evicted died. Of the 1 million or so casualties of the famine, most were evictees.

Evictions

The landlord was not present at evictions. Instead, he sent an agent, backed up by police or military, to deliver the bad news to the tenants. Fellow tenants, called drivers, followed up by intimidating the evictees and tossing out their possessions.

Several works of art depict the terrible scenes in which a destitute family was confronted by the landlord's agent, who was mounted on horseback. On bended knee, the tenants may have pleaded with him to let them stay. Perhaps an old woman would put a hex on the agent or curse the name of the landlord. Next, the drivers came to knock down the cottage. Whatever the evicted family could not carry was free for the scavengers to pick through. The family would be marched off the property and left at the crossroads. The process would often take less than 20 minutes.

A deadly spiral took hold of these unfortunate people. Starving was made worse by illness. In turn, this was made worse by the lack of shelter. As they slept out in the open or in caves, many of the evicted died from exposure to the cold, wind, and rain.

The British government knew the evictions caused mass suffering and death. In a few instances, Irish landlords and even the British government paid passage to send evictees to the United States or British North America (now Canada). The British intentionally did not undertake a wide-reaching program to promote emigration. According to Trevelyan, that "would do much real mischief by encouraging the Irish to rely upon the government for emigration."[5] Even without help, however, many Irish found their own way out of Ireland. They flocked to their island's ports to escape the suffering caused by nature and made tragic by misguided policies. ⌐

Many of those who were evicted ended up living in makeshift outdoor shelters.

Irish immigrants stream off a ship to find new lives in North America.

BOUND FOR
FOREIGN SHORES

uring the Great Famine, approximately
2 million people left Ireland for distant
shores. Those who could afford passage out of their
native land were of moderate means, usually tenant
farmers or urban merchants or tradesmen. They

were desperate to escape their broken country.

HEADED FOR AMERICA

The overwhelming majority of Irish left for North America, where opportunities seemed most plentiful. Nearly 1.5 million Irish arrived in the United States between 1845 and 1855. The port of New York alone, and the newly constructed immigration center at Castle Garden, received 651,931 passengers. The Irish also streamed into U.S. cities such as Boston, Philadelphia, New Orleans, and Chicago.

Passage to British North America (now Canada) was significantly cheaper than to the United States. This was because some landlords, charities, or even government agencies helped pay the cost of some tickets. Approximately 340,000 Irish sailed to what are now Canadian ports. U.S. officials, overwhelmed

A Big Business

Great Britain's Royal Navy was the largest in the world, and all its ships were made of wood. However, Great Britain, along with the rest of Europe, had been largely deforested since the Middle Ages. So the Royal Navy looked to the seemingly endless forests of what is now Canada for the wood it needed. With the Irish streaming into North America, the demand for trans-Atlantic crossings was high. Starting in 1815, many shipping companies saw a business opportunity. They outfitted their cargo ships with makeshift bunks. After unloading a shipment of lumber from North America on England's shores, the ships were loaded with Irish emigrants for the return voyage. At times, ferrying people to North America became more profitable than shipping timber to Great Britain.

by the numbers of Irish arriving in U.S. cities, hoped those passengers would stay put. At the insistence of the United States, many of these passengers were made to swear an oath that they would remain in British territory. However, little more than half did. The rest fled south to the United States. British North America was a wild, thinly populated territory with often-brutal weather. It offered few job prospects. Also, many Irish hated the idea of once again living under British rule.

The Journey

So many people wanted to escape Ireland that ships began sailing even in autumn and winter, braving fierce storms and icebergs. Only a few ships left Irish ports directly for America. It was more common, and usually less expensive, for passengers to take a ferry across the Irish Sea to Liverpool, England. Once they

Human Exports

Britain had a history of sending criminals overseas. Many convicts had been sent to penal colonies in North America or Australia. Men and women were sent to penal colonies for various crimes. These included petty theft, murder, and speaking out against the Crown. After the very long journey to the colonies, the convicts were forced into hard labor and received regular beatings. Many died after only a short time in a penal colony. During the famine years, some Irish people believed that being sent to Australia would be better than staying in Ireland. They intentionally committed crimes in order to be sent away.

arrived in England, passengers waited in crowded boarding houses, where they were prey to pickpockets and con artists. Finally, the passengers boarded large vessels bound for the United States or British North America.

The journey lasted 40 days or more, depending on the size and make of the ship and the weather. The voyage was cramped and uncomfortable. Each passenger was assigned a tiny space on a wooden bunk that was no wider than 18 inches (46 cm). Some ships were outfitted with as many as four rows of bunks from floor to ceiling.

The Hannah was a smaller ship. At 59 feet (18 m) long, it could easily fit inside a high school basketball court. Even so, 60 people were packed into the hull. Other triple-decker vessels had originally been built to carry mail. Now converted to carry people, they packed in as many as 400 per voyage.

The passengers could bring only what they could carry. Sometimes, if there was not enough room on board, families had to leave their belongings at the pier. Gangs of scavengers were always nearby to pick through the baggage left behind. Among the most important items to have on board were cooking pots. These allowed families to prepare their meals at sea, though rations of food and water were meager. Also important were a craftsman's tools or a spinning wheel. The Irish would need these items to make a living in America. Sometimes there was room for a fiddle or two, or a set of bagpipes.

The passengers spent most of their time below deck. In good weather, they might be allowed on deck to take in some fresh air. There was no way to wash in the ship's small, crowded hull, and disease spread very quickly. In bad weather, the ships rocked violently and caused seasickness. Also, when the water was rough, cooking was not allowed. Authorities feared that hot coals might roll away and cause a fire. Sometimes the ships leaked, which made the quarters damp. Women, who wore long dresses, faced a peculiar problem. At times, a woman might find her dress stuck between the ship's planks. She would have to stay in place, waiting for the ship's weight to shift before pulling herself free.

"Coffin Ships"

The ships are remembered as "coffin ships" because many passengers died of disease on the journey. The horrors of the coffin ships were generally confined to Black '47, when panic to leave

Ireland was at its height. Many of the 1847 passengers were ill when they boarded, and their illness easily spread in the dirty, crowded hulls.

Upon arrival, those who did survive were put in quarantine. They were separated from the public for weeks. This was to protect the city slums from any diseases the immigrants may have brought with them. Many Irish peasants, already weary from the trip, were kept aboard the ship during this time. Though they survived passage, many immigrants died on the docked ship during quarantine.

Tragedy in Quebec

For those sailing to British North America in 1847, a terrible fate awaited them before landing in Quebec. Immigrants arriving at the city were processed and quarantined at Grosse Île, an island in the St. Lawrence River. By May, as many as 40 ships lay at anchor in a row stretching approximately 2 miles (3 km). More than 21,000 passengers awaited permission to land. Famine-related diseases spread quickly among the weak, dirty, and crowded masses. The people were prevented from leaving the island for fear that the highly contagious diseases would spread on the mainland. From June through September, death tolls rose, and the Irish were buried in mass graves.

Today, a granite cross stands over the site of the burials. The memorial is inscribed with dedications in French, English, and Irish. The Irish words read:

Children of the Gael died in their thousands on this island having fled from the laws of the foreign tyrants and an artificial famine in the years 1847–48. God's loyal blessing upon them. Let this monument be a token to their name and the honour from the Gaels of America. God Save Ireland.[1]

Social activist and philanthropist Steven de Vere vividly described the horrors of a "coffin ship" of 1847:

Hundreds of poor people, men, women, and children of all ages, from the driveling idiot of ninety to the babe just born; huddled together without light, without air, wallowing in filth and breathing a fetid atmosphere, sick in body, dispirited in heart . . .; the fevered patients lying between the sound in sleeping spaces so narrow as almost to deny them the power of indulging, by a change in position, the natural restlessness of the diseased; by their agonised ravings disturbing those around them and predisposing them, through the effects of imagination, to imbibe the contagion; living without food or medicine except as administered by the hand of casual charity; dying without the voice of spiritual consolation, and buried in the deep without the rites of the church. [2]

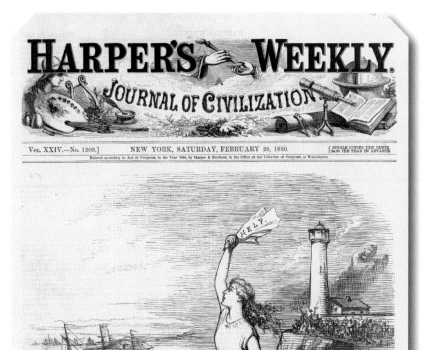

HARPER'S WEEKLY.

A JOURNAL OF CIVILIZATION

Vol. XXIV.—No. 1209.]   NEW YORK, SATURDAY, FEBRUARY 28, 1880.   [SINGLE COPIES TEN CENTS. | $4.00 PER YEAR IN ADVANCE.

Entered according to Act of Congress, in the Year 1880, by Harper & Brothers, in the Office of the Librarian of Congress, at Washington.

WE ARE STARVING

IRELAND

HELP.

THE *HERALD* OF RELIEF FROM AMERICA.

A U.S. magazine cover shows a woman on Ireland's shore. She is holding up a sign that says "help," at a time of another famine in the late 1800s.

*An Irish family gathers outside on a summer evening
in a New York City slum.*

THE IRISH IN AMERICA

Many passengers to the New World had been told exaggerated tales of the prosperity they would find in America. After a sorrowful parting from loved ones, they would often celebrate upon boarding the emigrant ships.

However, their hopes were soon dashed by the hardships of the voyage. Then, once on land, further troubles awaited them.

A HOSTILE RECEPTION

The Irish soon realized that life was hard for newcomers. U.S. attitudes toward the Irish differed little from the British. Many Americans believed that the Irish were drunken and dishonest thieves, looking to upset their way of life. U.S. citizens worried that the Irish would take their jobs. "Help Wanted" signs in shop windows and factories often had the initials N.I.N.A. written below. The dreaded letters stood for *No Irish Need Apply.* So the Irish immigrants ended up with the least-desirable jobs U.S. society had to offer.

As Irish-American author Frank McCourt stated:

New York Slums

In New York City, immigrants could afford to live only in crowded tenement buildings. Families of often five or more people crammed into one-room apartments. The buildings were built close together, so there was little airflow. The smell of garbage from the streets wafted throughout the building. The rooms were terribly hot in summer and mercilessly cold in winter. Families shared just one bathroom per floor, and it had no running water. Through the thin walls, one could hear mice and rats scratching. Every footstep and every baby's cry were clearly heard. Though many had lived in poor conditions in Ireland, the immigrants were not used to city life. Life in the slums deeply affected the morale of the newcomers.

The Know-Nothings

Some anti-Irish citizens formed a political party aimed at stopping the stream of immigrants into American ports. This party came to be known as the Know-Nothing Party during the 1850s.

The semisecret organization was open only to white, Protestant men. The name spurred the party motto, "I know only my country, my whole country, and nothing but my country."[2] Much of the group's activity was aimed at preventing Irish immigrants from obtaining jobs and citizenship. Official party goals included: stopping immigration from Catholic countries; allowing only Protestants to become school teachers; allowing only native-born citizens to hold public office; and promoting daily Bible readings from the Protestant version of the Bible, the King James Bible. The Know-Nothings never became a major political party and did not survive past the 1860s.

The Irish came to America . . . because they thought that the streets were paved with gold. But when we got here, we found out that not only weren't they paved with gold, they weren't paved at all. Furthermore we were expected to pave them, which we did.[1]

The Irish found lodging in city slums that were overcrowded, noisy, and dirty. Many of these immigrants came from Ireland's countryside. They had never lived in cities or towns before, so the New York slums must have been a shock. Because the Irish felt deeply unwelcome in their new country, they stuck together. Many settled near one another in densely populated Irish ghettos. They found some comfort in familiar surroundings—people who spoke the same way, ate the same kinds of foods, and understood the same culture. In turn, Irish ghettos made some U.S. citizens even more nervous. The United States was a

A racist cartoon from 1870 shows caricatures of an African American and an Irish American balanced on a scale.

mostly Protestant country. Some Protestants feared that the Catholic Irish were agents sent by the pope in Rome to take over the United States.

A STEADY RISE IN IMMIGRATION

One might think that discrimination the Irish faced in the United States would have discouraged other immigrants from coming. That proved not to be the case at all. In 1847, the U.S. Congress passed laws requiring better conditions on immigrant ships

Old St. Patrick's Church, Chicago

The oldest public building in Chicago—and one of the few buildings that survived the Great Chicago Fire of 1871—is Old St. Patrick's Catholic Church. The church was built by Irish immigrants in the 1850s. Old St. Patrick's was the center of Irish immigrant life in Chicago.

In 1912, to honor the church's Irish roots, artist Timothy O'Shaughnessy designed and built 15 stained glass windows for the site. The windows are based on designs from the medieval *Book of Kells*, an illustrated version of the four gospels created by Irish monks. Old St. Patrick's stands as an example of the Irish immigrants' dedication to their community and their esteem for their heritage—a heritage they had been forced to forsake.

coming into the country. According to some historians, these laws were not enacted by humane motives. They were passed to force an increase in the cost of ticket prices. The hope was to discourage Irish from coming to the United States, but the plan failed. Fares to U.S. ports did increase, but the Irish kept coming. The panic of Black '47 gave way to less fraught, more organized—and increased—immigration. Irish emigration to the United States continued in high numbers until well into the twentieth century. As late as the 1990s, more Irish came to the United States than did people migrating to Ireland from elsewhere.

Why did immigration continue to rise? Though the famine ended in 1852, fears of future famines and dissatisfaction with British rule continued to drive the Irish from their land. Also, by 1870, the U.S. economy was one of the fastest growing in the world. The promise of plentiful jobs and high wages helped persuade young Irish men and women to leave Ireland for the United States. As time went on, the Irish-American community grew vast. Chances were that an Irish immigrant already had relatives living in the United States.

IRISH AMERICANS

After years of desperate struggle, many Irish thrived in the United States. There was always hard labor to be done in the ever-expanding United States. The Irish dug canals. They built railroads and highways. The Irish moved westward, carving out new farms in the Midwest. In Chicago, the Irish butchered meat in slaughterhouses. In 1849, the California gold rush drew tens of thousands of Irishmen from the port cities in the East. Men accustomed to digging for spuds found the prospect of digging for gold enticing. The gold rush offered other opportunities as well. In San Francisco, the Irish opened up shops catering to gold miners. They worked the farms of the West Coast.

The Irish brewed beer with the Germans in Milwaukee and forged steel in Pittsburgh and Philadelphia. They helped to build New York's subway system as well as bridges, tunnels, canals, and railroads. They worked on iron beams high above the growing U.S. cities and in shipyards. In West Virginia, many Irish immigrants mined the coal that fired up U.S. industries.

DISTINGUISHED INDIVIDUALS

During the Civil War (1861–1865), Irish Americans fought on both sides of the war. However, because the recent waves of immigrants had settled in Northern states, higher numbers defended the Union. The 69th New York Infantry, or the "Fighting 69th," was made up entirely of Irish immigrants. The group distinguished themselves in the battles of Bull Run and Gettysburg. Thomas Francis Meagher was responsible for the formation of the brigade. Meagher also led the Fighting 69th after the Battle of Bull Run. And yet Meagher had fought all odds just to make it to the United States. Several years earlier, Meagher had been convicted by a British court of leading a failed rebellion in Ireland. He was sentenced to death. However, Queen Victoria changed his punishment, and exiled him to Australia. Meagher managed to escape and came to the United States.

The officers of the "Fighting 69th," photographed during the Civil War

Henry Ford was another noteworthy Irish American. His father, William, left Ireland in 1847 for Dearborn, Michigan. William and his wife, Mary, raised six children on a large farm. Born in 1863, Henry was the eldest. Even as a boy, Henry was fascinated by machines and gadgets. When he grew up, he left the family farm and sought his fortune in Detroit, Michigan. In 1903, he founded the Ford Motor Company. He built the Model T, the first automobile affordable enough for the average person. In the 1950s, the Ford Motor Company produced the popular Ford Fairlane. This model was named after Henry's estate in Dearborn, Michigan.

He had called his home Fair Lane after an area in County Cork, Ireland, where his foster grandfather had been born.

The Kennedy family has produced perhaps the most famous Irish Americans. During the Great Famine, Patrick and Bridget Kennedy left New Ross, County Wexford, and settled in Boston. Patrick Joseph Kennedy was

Irish Americans of Note

Some prominent Irish Americans include:
- Francis O'Neill (1848–1937)—Superintendent of the Chicago Police Department from 1901 to 1905 and a collector of Irish folk music
- Henry McCarty (Billy the Kid) (1859–1881)—The most famous outlaw of the Old West during the late nineteenth century
- Henry Ford (1863–1947)—Founder of Ford Motor Company
- Molly Brown (1867–1932)—*Titanic* survivor
- Leonora O'Reilly (1870–1927)—Trade union organizer
- Eugene O'Neill (1888–1953)—Playwright
- Richard J. Daley (1902–1976)—Mayor of Chicago from 1955 to 1976
- Bing Crosby (1903–1977)—Famous American singer and actor
- William J. Brennan (1906–1997)—U.S. Supreme Court Justice from 1956 to 1990
- John F. Kennedy (1917–1963)—Thirty-fifth president of the United States
- Mary Higgins Clark (b. 1927)—Novelist
- Maureen Dowd (b. 1952)—Journalist

the young couple's second son. He was the first of his family to receive a first-rate education. The ambitious young man looked for ways to make money. He started off owning a saloon that catered to recent Irish immigrants. By the 1880s, P. J., as he was called, had created a small fortune. He won a seat in the Massachusetts State House in 1884 and later went on to serve two terms in the state Senate.

P. J.'s eldest surviving son was Joseph Kennedy. Joseph became a successful businessman and an important figure in the Democratic Party. He also served as the U.S. Ambassador to the United Kingdom between 1938 and 1940. Joseph's son John Fitzgerald Kennedy became the first practicing Catholic and Irish American to become president of the United States. Joseph Kennedy's youngest son, Edward (Ted), has served as the senior U.S. senator from Massachusetts.

Perhaps the success of Irish Americans is best shown through the growth of Irish culture in America. The 1.5 million Irish men and women who came to the United States during the Great Famine changed the country's ethnic and cultural landscape. Today, more than 40 million U.S. citizens can boast of some Irish blood. Every year on March 17, thousands of parades and festivals are held in honor of Saint Patrick, the patron saint of Ireland. The day celebrates the history of the Irish in America. ⌐

Saint Patrick's Day

On March 17th, Irish Americans celebrate their heritage by participating in Saint Patrick's Day parades and festivals. Saint Patrick's Day is one of the most celebrated ethnic holidays in the United States, with nearly every major city hosting a public event. Some of the more famous parades are the New York Saint Patrick's Day parade and the Chicago South Side Irish parade. The day also offers a chance to listen to Irish music, watch Irish step dancing, and taste Irish foods. The holiday is not just for people of Irish descent. It is a time for people of all backgrounds to remember the sacrifices and sufferings of the Irish who sought opportunity in the United States—and to celebrate their success.

Teenage girls perform traditional Irish dance during the 2007 Chicago St. Patrick's Day Parade.

*In Ireland, the ruins of deserted stone cottages stand
as reminders of the Great Famine.*

THE LEGACY OF THE GREAT FAMINE

The Great Famine had a lasting impact on Ireland and its people. The famine drastically reduced the country's population. Also, droves of Irish citizens continued to leave their homeland for more than a century.

The famine drastically reduced Ireland's rural population. The wealthy landlords were able to consolidate their holdings at a great cost. The estates were in such poor shape and in such debt that they were no longer profitable. Also, a tremendous labor shortage existed throughout the land. Entire villages and towns were abandoned. It was in these small communities where Irish had been spoken. The famine struck a deathblow to the country's native language as well.

In the west, row after row of stone walls still mark off tiny plots on which Ireland's poorest families had once barely made their livings. The stone walls of their ruined cottages still stand. These are silent testaments of Ireland's great tragedy. The men and women who tended those tiny plots and the families who lived in those now-ruined homes escaped to the New World, if they were lucky. Most of them died from starvation or disease.

The Easter Rebellion

After the famine, the Irish were deeply dissatisfied with British rule. Hatred of British occupation came to a boiling point as the Irish called for their own, independent government. In 1914,

Patrick Pearse

The leader of the Easter Rebellion was born on November 10, 1879, in Dublin. Pearse's father was an immigrant from England. He came to Ireland to practice his trade as a stonemason on the country's many churches. As a boy, Pearse became infatuated with Irish language and culture. At 23, he became the editor of an Irish-language newspaper. Later, Pearse went on to found an Irish-language school. Pearse believed that the preservation of the Irish language was fundamental to the cause of Irish freedom. His love of his native country and its language led him to fight the British in 1916. Pearse was 36 when he was executed by a British firing squad on May 3, 1916.

the British officially granted self-rule to Ireland. However, the outbreak of World War I delayed actual self-rule. Anger at the delay resulted in the violent Easter Rebellion of 1916. On the Monday after Easter, April 24, 1916, Irish rebels rallied behind their leader, Patrick Pearse. They seized control of the Dublin post office and other strategic locations within the city. The next day, they proclaimed a free Irish republic.

The British government responded with force. It declared martial law throughout Ireland and sent in more soldiers. The British army and the Irish rebels fought bitterly. By April 29, the rebellion had been crushed. The rebels were dragged before a military court. There, they were quickly sentenced to death. Pearse and 15 other men were shot by a firing squad.

Pearse's execution inflamed the anger of the Irish and gave Ireland's

The Easter Rebellion of 1916 left parts of Dublin in ruins.

Nationalist Party, also known as *Sinn Féin,* a significant boost in popular support. In 1918, *Sinn Féin* won a landslide victory across Ireland for seats in the British Parliament. The elected officials refused to take their seats in London. Instead, they proclaimed Ireland independent from Great Britain and formed the Irish Assembly, the *Dáil Éireann.*

The Rise to Nationhood

The British government rejected the idea of an Irish republic. From 1919 to 1921, the Irish Republican Army (IRA) fought the British in a costly war for independence. Led by Michael Collins, the IRA used guerilla-war techniques against British agents and soldiers.

By June 1921, the British recognized that the war was becoming too damaging. Victory would cost an extreme loss of life and continued damage to its

Ireland Today

By the 1990s, Ireland had become one of the most economically vibrant countries in Europe. The country earned the nickname the "Celtic Tiger," as it became one of Europe's major centers for computer technology and manufacturing. Today, the Irish are prospering.

The Irish population sank to its lowest level in modern times in 1960, but it soon began to rebound. Also, the tide of immigration reversed starting in the mid-1990s, as Ireland's booming economy needed more and more workers. Immigrants from Poland, China, and Nigeria poured into Irish cities. The Irish government has also worked to increase citizenship. It has extended invitations to recent émigrés and their descendants to return to Ireland. In fact, anyone in the United States with at least one Irish parent or grandparent may apply for Irish citizenship.

In 2001, Ireland joined with much of mainland Europe in adopting the euro as its currency. In 2002, the euro became stronger than even the U.S. dollar. This has led to even more investment in Ireland's economy.

Some people feel Ireland's prosperity has a downside in that the country is losing some of its identity. Others present a more hopeful view. They argue that with its newfound wealth, Ireland can invest more in educating the world about Irish culture.

reputation. By now, Irish Americans held significant influence in U.S. politics, and the United States was a growing world power. Britain agreed to the formation of the Irish Free State on December 6, 1921. In 1949, Ireland declared itself a fully separate republic. At last, Ireland was completely independent from Great Britain.

From Tragedy to Triumph

The famine left a legacy in Ireland, but it also left one in the United States. The contributions made by the Irish who fled for North America are another lasting impact of the tragedy.

On June 28, 1998, more than 7,000 people gathered to dedicate the $1 million Boston Irish Famine Memorial. The memorial is near Downtown Crossing, close to where tens of thousands of Irish immigrants came to escape the Great Hunger.

"We declare the right of the people of Ireland to the ownership of Ireland, and to the unfettered control of Irish destinies. . . . [W]e hereby proclaim the Irish Republic as a Sovereign Independent State, and we pledge our lives and the lives of our comrades-in-arms to the cause of its freedom, of its welfare, and of its exaltation among the nations."[1]
—*The Proclamation of the Irish Republic, 1916*

More than 3 million people visit the memorial each year.

The site pays tribute to the hardships and hopes of the early Irish immigrants. It recognizes their story as an important chapter in U.S. history. Irish immigrants did eventually find opportunities. They also paved the way for future generations of immigrants from many countries around the world.

The memorial features two life-size sculptures. One shows an Irish family in agony from the Great Famine. The other shows a hopeful family arriving on U.S. shores. According to a 1998 editorial in the *Boston Globe,* the statue depicts "the odyssey of the Irish immigrant from tragedy to triumph over the past 150 years." It adds:

> *Beyond its particular Irish dimension, the memorial marks the beginning of the waves of 19th and 20th century immigration. . . . Thousands more would come: Italians, Jews, Greeks, Lithuanians, Chinese, Haitians, Dominicans, blacks from the American South, and other ethnic groups, all seeking . . . a refuge from poverty and oppression. The triumph of the Irish is a parable of America.*[2]

A woman stands vigil in front of the Boston Irish Famine Memorial.

TIMELINE

ca. 500 BCE	ca. 433	ca. 461
Celtic peoples invade Ireland and the British Isles.	Patrick returns to Ireland to teach Catholicism.	Patrick dies.

1815	1829	1845
The first Corn Laws are passed.	Catholic Emancipation ends the last of the Penal Laws.	In September, the *Gardener's Chronicle* reports that the potato blight has established itself firmly in Ireland.

1171	1695	1801
King Henry II of England invades Ireland.	The first Penal Laws are passed.	An Act of Union makes Ireland part of the United Kingdom.

1845	1845	1846
The British government sets up the Central Relief Commission to address the Irish potato famine in November.	In December, the *Freeman's Journal* reports that half of Ireland's potato crop is destroyed.	Robert Peel secures the repeal of the Corn Laws in June; Peel is forced to resign as prime minister.

TIMELINE

1846	1847	1847
In September, the potato crop fails across Ireland for the second year in a row.	Potato crops recover slightly in September.	Starting in September, British officials close soup kitchens; relief efforts focus on Irish workhouses.

1916	1922	1937
The Easter Rebellion is crushed by the British army on April 29; 16 rebels are executed.	The creation of the Irish Free State is ratified by the *Dáil Éireann* on January 7.	Ireland adopts its current constitution on December 29.

1847

Nearly 6,000 Irish émigrés die on la Grosse Île trying to gain entry into Quebec in the fall.

1848

The potato blight reappears in September.

1916

The Easter Rebellion breaks out in Dublin on April 24.

1949

On April 18, Ireland severs all remaining political ties with Great Britain and formally becomes a republic.

1961

In January, John Fitzgerald Kennedy becomes the thirty-fifth president of the United States.

1998

The Boston Irish Famine Memorial is dedicated on June 28.

ESSENTIAL FACTS

DATE OF EVENT

1845–1852

PLACE OF EVENT

Ireland

KEY PLAYERS

❖ Sir Robert Peel, prime minister of Great Britain at the start of the Great Famine

❖ Sir Charles Edward Trevelyan, Britain's assistant secretary of the treasury throughout the Great Famine, who headed the country's relief efforts in Ireland

HIGHLIGHTS OF EVENT

❖ The Irish masses were reduced to poverty as the result of hundreds of years of colonization by the British.

❖ By 1829, the vast majority of Irish worked on tiny plots of rented land. Many depended on a single crop—the potato—because it was able to grow in the country's poorest soil.

❖ A mysterious disease, later known to be caused by a fungus, caused Ireland's potato crops to rot beginning in 1845.

❖ British relief efforts were severely inadequate. They were hampered by political and economic ideas of the time. Ideas of laissez-faire capitalism justified England's stance of "non-interference" in Ireland's economy. Even though Irish soil continued to produce oats and other crops, the food was largely unavailable to the common peasant. Also, racist ideas about the Irish character placed responsibility for relief on the ravaged people themselves. Workhouses become houses of mass death.

❖ The famine took approximately 1 million lives, either directly from starvation or from related diseases. More than 2 million people emigrated from Ireland, mostly to the United States. The famine put in place a negative population growth. By the late twentieth century, Ireland's population was half of what it had been before the famine.

❖ Initially, Irish immigrants faced extreme hardship in the United States, but they continued to arrive in droves. Today, Irish Americans thrive.

QUOTE

"That one million people should have died in what was then part of the richest and most powerful nation in the world is something that still causes pain as we reflect on it today. Those who governed in London at the time failed their people through standing by while a crop failure turned into a massive human tragedy. We must not forget such a dreadful event." —*Tony Blair, the British prime minister, speaking in 1997*

ADDITIONAL RESOURCES

SELECT BIBLIOGRAPHY

Donnelly, James S. Jr. *The Great Irish Potato Famine.* Thrupp, Stroud, Gloucestershire: Sutton Publishing, 2001.

Foster, R. F., ed. *The Oxford History of Ireland.* Oxford, New York: Oxford University Press, 2001.

Gallagher, Carole S. *The Irish Potato Famine.* Philadelphia: Chelsea House Publishers, 2002.

Laxton, Edward. *The Famine Ships: The Irish Exodus to America.* New York: Henry Holt and Company, 1997.

Mitchel, John. *The Last Conquest of Ireland (Perhaps).* Glasgow, 1876.

Ó Gráda, Cormac. *Black '47 and Beyond: The Great Irish Famine in History, Economy, and Memory.* Princeton, NJ: Princeton University Press, 2000.

Trevelyan, Charles Edward. *The Irish Crisis.* London: Longman, Brown, Green & Longmans, 1848.

FURTHER READING

Bartoletti, Susan Campbell. *Black Potatoes: The Story of the Great Irish Famine, 1845–1850.* Boston: Houghton Mifflin, 2001.

Dolan, Edward F. *The Irish Potato Famine: The Story of Irish-American Immigration.* New York: Benchmark Books, 2003.

Gallagher, Carole S. *The Irish Potato Famine.* Philadelphia: Chelsea House Publishers, 2002.

Haugen, Brenda. *The Irish-Americans.* Philadelphia: Mason Crest, 2003.

Web Links

To learn more about the Irish potato famine, visit ABDO Publishing Company online at **www.abdopublishing.com**. Web sites about the Irish potato famine are featured on our Book Links page. These links are routinely monitored and updated to provide the most current information available.

Places to Visit

Boston Irish Famine Memorial Project
50 Braintree Hill Office Park, Braintree, MA 02184
781-849-4444
www.boston.com/famine/index.html
The Project keeps alive the memory of the Irish famine victims through the operation of a park and sculpture in downtown Boston.

Grosse Île and Irish Memorial National Historic Site of Canada
2 D'Auteuil Street, P.O. Box 10, Station B, Québec, Québec G1K 7A1, Canada
888-773-8888
www.pc.gc.ca/lhn-nhs/qc/grosseile/index_e.asp
The site features a memorial with all the known names of those who died in quarantine on the island or on boats stationed off the coast.

The Irish Hunger Memorial
Battery Park, Vesey Street and North End Avenue, New York, NY 10382
212-417-2000
www.batteryparkcity.org/page/page3_2.html
The memorial features the remains of an Irish stone house among native Irish plants.

GLOSSARY

Black '47
The name given to the deadliest year of the Great Famine, 1847.

blight
A generic term for a disease that infects plants.

Catholic
A member of the Roman Catholic Church; most Irish people were and are professed Catholics.

Celts
An ancient, warring group of people from Europe and Asia minor; Celtic culture was at its height from the fifth through first centuries BCE.

colony
An area controlled by an outside country.

conacre
An arrangement whereby a plot of land is hired out to laborers to grow a food crop.

dysentery
A deadly and highly contagious disease resulting in painful diarrhea and intestinal bleeding.

emigrate
To leave one's own country in order to live in another.

empire
A political unit made up of many different nations and colonies ruled over by one government with supreme power.

European Union
An organization of European countries that work together in many areas, including economics and politics.

evict
To legally force someone off a piece of property.

famine
A lengthy and severe lack of food, usually due to a natural disaster along with economic and political factors.

genocide
> The intentional elimination by murder of members of a particular race of people.

Goidelic
> The earliest Celtic language variant spoken in Ireland.

laissez-faire
> An economic philosophy that eliminates government interference in commerce; French for "let him do as he will."

moralism
> The belief that Irish poverty and the Great Famine were the results of a moral defect in the Irish people.

N.I.N.A.
> A terms that stands for "No Irish Need Apply," a phrase found on many help-wanted signs in the United States during the period of mass Irish immigration.

Protestant
> A member of a Christian sect whose religious ideals were founded in response to perceived abuses by the Roman Catholic Church.

tuber
> The edible portion of a root of some vegetables used to store extra nutrients and sugars for the plant to use during winter or while seeding.

United Kingdom
> A European country that includes Great Britain (England, Wales, and Scotland) and Northern Ireland; Ireland was part of the United Kingdom until it became independent in 1921.

wake
> A vigil held in the presence of a recently deceased person; during a wake, mourners may pray, tell stories, sing, and eat and drink.

SOURCE NOTES

Chapter One: A Devastating Tragedy
1. "Cherishing the Irish Diaspora: Address to the House of
Oireachtas by President Mary Robinson." *The Irish Emigrant.* 2 Feb.
1995. 1 May 2008 <http://www.emigrant.ie/emigrant/historic/
diaspora.htm>.
2. Michael Pollack. "Sites Remember the Irish Potato Famine." *The
New York Times.* 15 March 2000. 1 May 2008 <http://www.irishside.
com/tis/content/nyt/130.htm>.

Chapter Two: History of Ireland
None

Chapter Three: On the Brink of Disaster
None

Chapter Four: *An Spáinneach,* the Potato
1. Sir John Forster. *England's Happiness Increased: A Sure and Easy Remedy
Against All Succeeding Dear Years by a Plantation of the Roots Called Potatoes.*
London, 1664. 1–2.
2. Cormac Ó Gráda. *Black '47 and Beyond: The Great Irish Famine in History,
Economy, and Memory.* Princeton, NJ: Princeton University Press,
1999. 14.
3. "A Short History of Ireland." *bbc.co.uk.* 1 May 2008 <http://www.
bbc.co.uk/northernireland/ashorthistory/archive/intro182.shtml>.

Chapter Five: *An Gorta Mór*, the Great Hunger

1. James Donnelly. *The Great Irish Potato Famine*. Thrupp, Stroud, Gloucestershire: Sutton Publishing, 2001. 44.

2. "Irish in Ireland: Newspapers." *bbc.co.uk*. 1 May 2008 <http://www.bbc.co.uk/scotland/education/int/hist/immigrants/irish_in_ireland/newspapers_irish_ireland.shtml>.

3. Cormac Ó Gráda. *Black '47 and Beyond: The Great Irish Famine in History, Economy, and Memory*. Princeton, NJ: Princeton University Press, 1999. 40.

4. "Give Me Three Grains of Corn, Mother." *Digital Tradition Mirror*. 1 May 2008 <http://sniff.numachi.com/pages/tiGRANCORN;ttTHREEGRN.html>.

5. "Famine Poetry." Nebraska Department of Education. 11 June 2008 <http://www.nde.state.ne.us/SS/irish/unit_7.html>.

Source Notes Continued

Chapter Six: Great Britain's Role
1. Cecil Woodham-Smith. *The Great Hunger: Ireland (1845–1849)*.
London: Harper & Row, 1962. 159.
2. James Donnelly. *The Great Irish Potato Famine*. Thrupp, Stroud,
Gloucestershire: Sutton Publishing, 2001. 18.
3. Peter Gray. *Famine, Land and Politics: British Government and Irish
Society, 1843–1850*. Dublin: Irish Academic Press, 1999. 331.
4. James Donnelly. *The Great Irish Potato Famine*. Thrupp, Stroud,
Gloucestershire: Sutton Publishing, 2001. 22.
5. Ibid. 32.

Chapter Seven: Bound for Foreign Shores
1. Tim Pat Coogan. *Wherever Green Is Worn: The Story of the Irish Diaspora*.
New York: Random House, 2000. 374.
2. James Donnelly. *The Great Irish Potato Famine*. Thrupp, Stroud,
Gloucestershire: Sutton Publishing, 2001. 180.

Chapter Eight: The Irish in America
1. Ron Wertheimer. "Television Review: When Irish Eyes Are Smiling . . . And Not." *The New York Times*. 16 Mar. 1999. 1 May 2008 <http://query.nytimes.com/gst/fullpage.html?res=9F0DEE D6103EF935A25750C0A96F958260>.
2. Frank H. Severance, ed. *Millard Fillmore Papers*. Buffalo, NY: The Buffalo Historical Society, 1907. 4.

Chapter Nine: The Legacy of the Great Famine
1. "Declaration of Independence." Spirited Ireland. 1 May 2008 <http://www.spirited-ireland.net/articles/declaration-of-independence>.
2. "Praise for the Memorial." Boston Irish Famine Memorial. 1 May 2008 <http://www.boston.com/famine/live.html>.

INDEX

ABOUT THE AUTHOR

Joseph R. O'Neill is a historian, author, and freelance journalist living in Los Angeles, California. He holds a BA in classics and history from Illinois' Monmouth College and an MA in ancient history from the University of Illinois. He has also studied at the University of Toronto, Canada, and the American School of Classical Studies in Athens, Greece. He has written several books and articles on a range of historical and literary topics and was a contributing author for the *Encyclopedia of the Ancient Greek World* (2006).

PHOTO CREDITS